Discourses on Practical Issues

John Owen

Vintage Puritan Series
GLH Publishing
Louisville, KY

Originally Titled *Several Practical Cases of Conscience Resolved*.
Sourced from *The Works of John Owen*. Vol. 9.
Edited by William Goold. Robert Carter & Brothers, New York, 1851.

ISBN:
Paperback 978-1-64863-066-8
Epub 978-1-64863-067-5

*For information on new releases, weekly deals,
and free ebooks visit*
www.GLHpublishing.com

DISCOURSES

Prefatory Note 1

I. Conviction of Sin 4

II. Evidence of an Interest in Christ 9

III. Concern of Christians in Public and National Sins 15

IV. Recovery from Spiritual Decay 22

V. The Ground of an Application to Christ 30

VI. How to Apply to Christ for Grace 36

VII. On Faith as to the Answer of Prayer 42

VIII. When is Sin Habitually Prevalent? 47

IX. Is Habitual Sin Consistent with Grace? 56

X. How to Deal with Prevailing Sin 64

XI. Christian Duty in Dark Dispensations 68

XII. Preparation for the Coming of Christ 79

XIII. The Contest between Christ and Antichrist 86

XIV. Christian Duty under Divine Warnings 89

PREFATORY NOTE

THESE brief Discourses are included in the folio edition of Owen's Sermons, published in 1721, and are there, for obvious reasons, made to occupy a place by themselves. They were delivered at church meetings for the purposes of devotion and conference among Christian brethren; and they relate to a particular department of Christian ethics. CASUISTRY — the science and doctrine of conscience — is designed, as the name denotes, to resolve *cases* of doubt and uncertainty in regard to points of subjective morality. As a branch of theological inquiry and discussion, it has in a great measure fallen into disrepute. It came to be regarded with suspicion and odium from the use made of it by the Jesuits in the fifteenth and sixteenth centuries, who converted it into an engine of successful villany. It was denounced as "the art of quibbling with God;" and it was partly the casuistical system of the Jesuits against which Pascal, in his "Provincial Letters," launched with scathing effect the bolts of his brilliant sarcasm.

But this science was for a time in great favour with the divines of the Reformation also; though studied and taught by them on different principles, and assuredly for very different ends. May-er, a German theologian of the Lutheran Church (1650–1712), in his "Bibliotheca Biblica," has a list of the authors on Casuistry under three divisions, comprehending the Calvinistic, Lutheran, and Romish Churches. The science was at one time extensively cultivated in England, and by divines of eminent reputation. Sanderson, bishop of Lincoln after the Restoration, has two works on it, — "Casus Conscientiæ," and "De Obligatione Conscientiæ Prælectiones." The "Ductor Dubitantium" of Jeremy Taylor is widely known as one of the most learned and important works on this subject. Baxter's "Christian Directory" deserves also to be, mentioned. Pike and Hayward's "Cases of Conscience" is a work that has been extensively circulated. There is a quarto volume in Latin entitled "Therapeutica Sacra," in which cases of conscience are discussed, by David Dickson, a Scotch divine, who, about 1650, was translated from the professorship of divinity in the University of Glasgow to the same chair in the University of Edinburgh. Four volumes of "The Morning Exercises" are occupied with the discussion and resolution of cases of conscience.

Casuistry is liable to abuse, and has often been abused. It tends to foster a morbid subjectivity, and to enervate principle. Every Christian pastor, however, in the course of his official duties, must sometimes be called to resolve the doubts and scruples which are apt to embarrass the tender conscience. As handled by the divines to whom we have last referred, it really embraces all questions of Christian obligation and practice; and on some points their discussions are among the best treatises on practical religion in the language. Nor can the divine entirely overlook casuistry, even in the strict sense of the term, seeing the apostle Paul was very careful to direct and enlighten the consciences of Christians in his day, who scrupled to eat "things offered in sacrifice unto idols."

It would be matter of regret, if the prejudice now entertained against a field of theological discussion cultivated to such an extent by divines of former generations, should prevent any reader from perusing the Discourses of our author which follow. Owen's was not the mind on any subject to be lost in obscure mysticism and refined subtilties, and to disport itself in a species of moral gymnastics, from which no overt and positive advantage could accrue to himself or to his hearers. These Discourses deal with momentous questions of religious experience, and are replete with suggestions and advices, which will be prized in proportion as the religion of the heart prevails, and so long as Christianity is not buried in formalism. The spirit which pervades all these brief but important Discourses, may be gathered from a weighty observation in one of them: "Suppose we should resolve with great earnestness, diligence, watchfulness, to abide in duties, in inward duties, to watch over our hearts, — which is required of us; yet if in our so doing we are taken off thereby from frequent actings of faith upon Christ, as the spring of our life, we shall decay, under all our endeavours, watchfulness, and multiplication of duties." — Ed.

I. Conviction of Sin[1]

QUESTION. *What conviction of a state of sin, and of the guilt of sin, is necessary to cause a soul sincerely to look after Christ?*

ANSWER. There is one thing only that I shall at present speak to, and that is this: What is the lowest condition that hath the nature of conviction in sincerity, so as that souls may not be discouraged from closing with Christ because they have had no greater convictions of sin? And I shall speak to it on this account, — because, although the things that have already been spoken by others are true, and such as those who have spoken them have found to be true by the word and their own experience; yet, it may be, others have not come up in their experience unto such a distinct observation of the work of conviction as hath been laid down, [so] that they may be discouraged. For, seeing conviction is so indispensably necessary, some may say, "It hath not been thus and thus with me, — according as hath been declared." Therefore, I would only show what I judge to be so necessary, as that without it a soul cannot be supposed sincerely to have closed with Christ. And we having all made our profession of choosing and closing

---

[1] Delivered January 28, 1672.

with Christ, as I would be loath to say any thing that might discourage any, lest they should have failed in the very necessary work of conviction; so I would not betray the truth of God, nor the souls of any.

Therefore, I shall place it upon this: What Jesus Christ doth indispensably call men unto, in order to believing in him, that is indispensably required of them. And this I shall manifest out of two or three places of Scripture:— Mark ii. 17, "I came not to call the righteous, but sinners to repentance." Now, this calling them unto repentance, is a calling them unto it by the faith which is in him. The apostle saith, 1 Tim. i. 15, "It is a faithful saying, and worthy of all acceptation, that Jesus Christ came into the world to save sinners." What kind of sinners doth Christ call? Whom he calls to repentance, he calls to faith; and whom he calls to faith, that they may truly believe, they are sinners, — opposed unto them that are righteous: "I came not to call the righteous, but sinners to repentance." "The righteous!" who are those righteous? The Scriptures tell us of these very men, that there were two sorts of them: First, Such as trusted in themselves that they were righteous, and despised other men. As long as a man trusteth in himself that he is righteous, Christ doth not call that man to believe. So long as a man is persuaded that his condition is good enough, he shall do well enough, that man hath no warrant to believe. Another description of these very persons, though upon another occasion, is given by the apostle Paul, Rom. x. 3, where he says, they were ignorant of the righteousness of God, and went about to establish their own righteousness. Though they did not come to trust in themselves for righteousness, yet sought righteousness as it were by the works of the law, and went about to establish their own righteousness; — Jesus Christ doth not call these men to believe: these righteous persons have no ground for believing. What is the conclusion? "Lost sinners," saith Christ, "this is that I require of you." So that this is what I assert to be indispensably necessary, — namely, that they are so far convinced that they are sinners as to state and course, that they are not righteous in themselves, and can have no righteousness in themselves. I say, therefore, when a person is not really convinced that he is not righteous, he is not under the call of Jesus Christ; and if he doth believe this, he is under a sovereign dispensation, and let not such despond.

Another direction of Christ is, "They that be whole need not a physician, but they that are sick," Matt. ix. 12. There are, in my apprehension, two things in a sick person that have need of a physician: First, He hath an uneasiness. A man who is sick, though he would shift it, yet his uneasiness will cause him to send for a physician. Saith Christ, "I come to such persons who say they can find no rest nor ease in their present condition." It may be they have often tried this and that, and see all will not do, — they are sick still; conscience reflects, and their hearts are burdened, and they must have relief, or they shall not be free. Secondly, There is a fear that it will end in death. This puts the sick person upon sending for a physician. When the soul is made uneasy in its state and condition, can find no rest nor ease, it thinks, "If I abide here, I shall be lost for ever." This soul doth Christ call; this man will be at the charge of a physician, cost what it will.

There is another word of Christ [which] very remarkably speaks just to the same purpose, Matt. xi. 28, "Come unto me, all ye that labour and are heavy laden, and I will give you rest," — a soul finding itself under want, labouring after something whereby it may be accepted with God. I will not confine this to extraordinary instances, for sometimes he is found of them that sought him not; but the ordinary case of a labouring soul, before closing with Christ, is to abstain from sin, pray more or less, be found in duties, and under strong desires to be accepted with God. And what is the end of these labours and endeavours? They labour and are weary; — that is, they see their labour comes to no effect; they do not find rest, and peace, and acceptance with God. And here is the turning point; Isa. lvii. 10, "Thou art wearied in the greatness of thy way; yet saidst thou not, There is no hope." When the soul hath laboured for acceptance with God, and comes to be weary, saith Christ, "Come unto me." "No," saith the light of nature, "come unto me; trust unto your own endeavours." Saith the soul, "I will try what it will do; I will not say, 'There is no hope.'" Saith another, "I will not say so; I will go unto Christ:" — this is he whom Christ calls.

Now, these things I do account indispensably necessary, antecedently to believing, as to the substance of them. And this, I hope, hath been found in all our souls. And if we have obtained so far, we need not then question whether our closing with

Christ be sincere or not. This is all that I dare assert to be absolutely and indispensably necessary. Many pretend to believe, though they never were convinced thoroughly that they were not righteous, — never were sick in their lives, — never had fears that they should die. These are contrary to the express rule Christ hath given, "I came not to call the righteous, but sinners;" — not those that say, "There is hope," but those that say, "There is no hope."

II. Evidence of an Interest in Christ[2]

QUESTION. *Seeing the act of closing with Christ is secret and hidden, and the special times and seasons of our conversion unto God are unknown unto most, what are the most certain evidences and pledges that we have cordially and sincerely received Christ, and returned unto God?*

ANSWER. I do acknowledge the inquiry is very large, and such as we may be straitened in, through the abundance of it. I shall only speak plainly some few things that to me are an evidence of a sincere closing with Christ, and receiving of Christ, — such as I know have been of use unto some.

First. When there is a permanency and abiding in the choice we have made of Christ, notwithstanding opposition against it that we shall be sure to meet withal. I do not speak to the nature of the choice, or the means of it, — how the mind is prepared for it; but I speak unto the poorest, the weakest of the flock, that may be inquiring whether they have made a sincere choice of Christ or not: I say, they may try it by the permanency and abiding in their choice against opposition.

---

[2] Delivered February 7, 1672.

And there are two sorts of oppositions that will try us and shake us, as to our choice, as I have found it, if I have had any experience of these things — 1. Opposition from charges of the guilt of sin and the law. 2. Opposition from temptations unto sin:—

1. There will, even after sincere believing and closing with Christ, be many a heavy charge brought against a soul from the law, and the guilt of sin in the conscience. Now, in such a case, the inquiry is, What the soul abides by when it is shaken? Why, truly, if a man go only upon mere convictions, on such shaking impressions of the guilt of sin, he will be very ready and inclined in his own mind to tack about to some other relief. He puts out fair for his voyage, — the storm arises, — the ship will not carry him; — he must tack about for another harbour. I have known it so with some; and experienced, when the wind hath set very strong that way with myself, — when the guilt of sin hath been charged with all its circumstances, — the soul hath been very hardly able to keep its hold, yet notwithstanding resolved, "I will trust to Christ:" but it hath been tacking about to self again, — "I must remedy this, — have relief for this from myself; I cannot abide by it, and live wholly upon Christ; and when the storm is over, then I will out to sea again." I say, this is no good sign to me when things are so; but when a soul in all those charges that sometimes come upon it abides the issue, — "Here I will trust upon Christ, let the worst come upon me;" — this I call a permanency in our choice against opposition. I hope you have experience of it.

2. There must be a permanency in our choice of Christ against temptations unto sin, as well as against the charges from sin. Truly, the former — of abiding with Christ against the charges from sin — is our daily work: it is sometimes more high and pressing, but it is our daily work. But there are also temptations unto sin, — it may be to the neglect of our duty, or to a compliance in any evil way (which we are subject unto while in the body); and perhaps great sins. Here Joseph's reply, applied to Christ, is that which doth argue our choice of Christ to be sincere, — "How shall I do this great wickedness, and sin against God?" When the soul can draw a prevailing argument from that, "How shall I do this, and relinquish my Lord Christ?" — "I will not do this against him whom I have chosen," — this is a good argument, if frequently reiterated, that our choice of Christ is sincere.

Secondly. Growing up in a love unto the person of Christ is a great evidence to me of a sincere choice of Christ. It is a blessed field that is before me, but I shall but hint things unto you. When the soul hath received Christ, it cannot but study Christ; and though it is no argument against the sincerity of a man's faith and grace, that he doth principally regard the offices and graces of Christ, and the benefits we have by him, yet it is an argument against the thrift and growth of it: for a thriving faith and grace will come to respect principally the person of Christ. I mean this; — when the soul studies the person of Christ, — the glory of God in him, — of his natures, the union of them in one person, — of his love, condescension and grace;

and the heart is drawn out to love him, and cry, "Doubtless I count all things but loss and dung for the excellency of Christ Jesus my Lord." "What is thy beloved more than another beloved?" "My beloved is white and ruddy, the chiefest among ten thousand; he is altogether lovely." To see an excellency, a desirableness in the person of Christ, so as to grow in admiration and love of him, is to me an evidence that, when all fails besides, will greatly support the soul, and persuade it that its choice is true. Nay, it is one of the most spiritual evidences; for I much question whether an unregenerate man can love Christ for his own sake at all. But it is a good sign of growth, when our love to the person of Christ grows, when we meditate much upon it, and think much about it. I could show you wherein the beauty of Christ's person doth much consist; but I have not time now to do it.

Thirdly. Another evidence to me of the soul's having made a sincere choice of Christ is, when it continues to approve, judge well of, and every day more and more to see, the glory, the excellency, the holiness, the grace, which is in the way of salvation by Jesus Christ; approves of it as not only a necessary way, — a way it has betaken itself to, because it must unavoidably perish in any other way, — but when it approves of it to be a most excellent way, in pardoning sin freely through the atonement he hath made, and the imputation of his righteousness unto us, — while the righteousness, the holiness, and the grace of God in all this is glorified. Saith the soul, "What a blind, wretched creature was I, that I did not see an excellency in this way before! It is better than the way of the law and the old covenant. I approve of this way with all my heart. If all other ways were set before me, and made possible, I would choose this way, of going to God by Jesus Christ, as the best way, — that brings most glory to God and most satisfaction unto the creature, and is most suited to the desires of my heart, I would have no other way. 'I am the way, the truth, and the life,' says Christ; and this I will abide by, whatsoever becomes of me," replies the soul; "though I should perish, I will abide by it, since God hath given me such a discovery of the glory of saving sinners by Christ, that is inferior to nothing but the glory of heaven. I see that glory to God in it, — that exaltation to Christ, whom I would love, — that honour to the Holy Spirit, and safety to my own soul, — that I will abide by it." A growing in the approbation of this way gives some assurance that we have made a true and sincere choice of Christ.

Give me leave to add this one thing more: —

Fourthly. That a delight in obedience unto God by Christ, in the ways of his own appointment, is a great evidence that we have chosen Christ, and he us; — chosen him as our king, prophet, and priest. The ways of the worship of God in his church and ordinances, are the ways and worship of God in Christ, which he hath appointed. Take these things abstractedly and in themselves, and we should be apt to say of them, as was said of Christ, "There is no beauty in them, nor glory, that they should be desired." There is much more outward beauty and glory in other ways, that Christ hath not appointed. But if we love the ways Christ hath appointed, because he hath appointed them, then we choose those ways because we have chosen him to be our king; and that is it which gives them beauty and life. And when the ways of Christ's appointment grow heavy and burdensome to us, we are weary of them, and are willing to have our neck from under the yoke, — it is a sign we grow weary of him who is the author of them; and this is a great sign that we never made a right and sincere choice of him.

Many other things might be offered as evidences of sincere closing with Christ; but these are some which have been of use to me: and I hope they may be so unto some of you.

III. Concern of Christians in Public and National Sins

QUESTION. *What concern have we in the sins of the day wherein we live?*

ANSWER. All sins may be referred to two heads:— First, Irreligion. Secondly, Immorality.

First. Irreligion; and that may be reduced to two heads, — atheism and false worship: you may add, also, particularly, the contempt of all instituted worship. It takes up much of the sins against the first table; however, at present I shall only speak of the first of them:—

As to atheism, then, it may be no age can parallel that wherein we live, considering all the ways whereby the atheism of man's heart may discover itself. For, take it absolutely, and in the seat of it, it is found only in the heart of man; unless some one or other prodigious instance breaks out sometime, as we have had in our days: but otherwise, "The fool hath said in his heart, There is no God." The heart is the seat of atheism. But we consider the ways whereby this atheism may and doth manifest itself:—

(1.) By horrid, cursed, blasphemous swearing; which is a contempt of the name of God. And when did it ever more abound in this nation?

(2.) By reproaching of the Spirit of God. Perhaps this is the peculiar sin of the nation at this day; and that the like hath not been known or heard of in any nation under the sun.

(3.) By scoffing at all holy things; — at the Scriptures, — at every thing that carries a reverence and fear of God; so that a man who dares profess a fear of God in what he doth, makes himself a scorn.

(4.) Contempt of all God's providential warnings is another proof of atheism. Never had a nation more warnings from God's providence, nor ever were they more despised. These things, brethren, are not done in a corner; they are perpetrated in the face of the sun. The steam of them darkens the whole heaven, and they abound more and more every day.

Secondly. Shall we go to the other head, — namely, Immorality, — and see how it is there? It would be an endless thing, to go over the sins that reign among us: oppression, blood, uncleanness, sensuality, drunkenness, — all to the height, raging and reigning in the nation. I mention these things as a matter to be bewailed before the Lord by us this day; and we ought to be affected with the consideration of them.

Unto this great prevalency and predominancy of sin in the whole nation, there is added a strange and unspeakable security. The truth is, men were a little awakened one while in the nation. When the judgments of God — the pestilence, the fire, the sword, and the year after, another warning from heaven — were upon us, then there was a little awakening, like a man out of a dead sleep, that lifts up his head, and rubs his eyes for a time.

But I can say this, that it is now towards forty years since God enabled me to observe something in the world; and, to my knowledge, I never observed this nation in that state of security wherein it is at this day. For, even in former times, there were warnings continually that God had a controversy with the nation; and those that had any fear of God spake one to another about it; and we saw and found their warnings were not in vain. But here is now a general security. Men complain of straits, want, poverty, and the like; but as to any thing wherein God hath to do with the world, either my observation doth greatly deceive me, or I never saw, I think, so general a security as at this day in this nation. And this security hath reached us all, — even the churches of God themselves.

These things are matter of fact. The whole question is, Whether we are greatly to be concerned in these things or not? "They are the sins of wicked men, and they are the sins of the persecutors of God's people, and the like; and what have we to do with them?"

The psalmist of old said, that "rivers of waters ran down his eyes, because men did not keep the law of God." And you know that God doth set a special mark upon those, not that are free from the abominations of the age, but upon those that mourn for the abominations that are in the midst of us. It will not be enough for us, that we are free from those abominations, unless we are found to mourn for them. Brethren, our own hearts know we are guilty in this matter, and that we had need seek the face of God this day to give us a deeper sense of these things than we have obtained. The name of God is blasphemed, the Spirit of God reproached, a flood of iniquity spreads itself over the nation, the land of our nativity, over the inheritance of Christ, over a nation professing the reformed religion; — all things go backward, — every thing declines. Indeed, brethren, if you will not, I do acknowledge here before you, and to my own shame, I have great guilt upon me in this matter, that I have not been sensible of the abominations of the nation, so as to mourn for them and be humbled for them, as I ought to have been. And you will do well to search your hearts, and consider how it is with you; — whether indeed you have been affected with these things; or whether you have not thought all is well, while all hath been well with yourselves and families, and, it may be, with the church, that may have no trouble upon that account. The security that is upon the nation is dismal; and, I may say, I see no way or means whereby the nation should be freed from this security. The conduct of the ministry, which they are under generally, is not able to free them from this security; nor the dispensation of the word: [so] that it seems to be a security from God to lead on the nation to judgment; the means for the removal of it and the awakening of us being laid aside. And if it comes this way, or that way, any way, though we see not the morning of it, you will find yourselves concerned in it. — "Who may abide the day of his coming?"

We may do well, brethren, to consider the state of the church of God in the world, among ourselves, and our own condition. I need not tell you how it is in the world; but this I can say, that to my apprehensions, the interest of Christ and the gospel was never so fast going down in the world since it came into it, as at this day. I will give you my reason of what I say: When the gospel was first planted and brought into the world, the devil was not able to bring the church into its apostasy, under six, or seven, or eight hundred years, and that by degrees. Since the time of the Reformation, the church was progressive for about seventy years; it stood at a stay about the same proportion of time; and ever since, it hath been going backward, straitened in all places: the power of it decays, and the peace of it is taken away, and destruction everywhere seems to lie at the door. Many, indeed, are in great misery and distress: some I have heard of lately sold for slaves,[3] for the testimony of their conscience. How is it with the church of Christ in this nation? Truly, some [are] in great poverty, in great affliction, in great distress; and I am afraid we and others have not hearts to relieve them, as we ought to do, in a due manner: however, let us help them with our prayers. And that which is worst of all, there seems to me, I must acknowledge it, to be a very great decay in all churches of Christ

---

3 No date is assigned to this discourse. It was about the time, however, in which these discourses seem to have been delivered, that many of the Scottish Covenanters were banished. They were crowded into vessels bound for the West Indies or North America; and, after enduring fearful sufferings on the passage, were sold, when they reached Jamaica or Carolina, to work as slaves on the plantations. By refinement of cruelty, it was provided that this punishment should be reserved for "such rebels as were penitent"! From the language of Owen, it would seem that he alludes to some occurrences that had taken place at a distance, and not within the sphere of his own observation. It is probable, therefore, that he refers to the proceedings of the government in Scotland. — ED.

in the nation, especially among those of us who have had most peace, most prosperity. That which we call zeal for God is almost quite lost among us. Some of us have almost forgot whether there be such a thing as the cause and interest of Christ in the world. We who have cried and prayed about it, and had it upon our hearts, have sat down in our narrow compass, and almost forgot there is such a thing as the interest of Christ in the world, so as to have an active zeal for the ordinances of God according to rule, as God requires of us. Our primitive love, — how is it decayed! Value of the ordinances of Christ, and the society of his people for edification, — how cold are we grown in these things! How little is the church society upon our hearts, which some of us remember when it was the very joy of our souls! Truly we have reason to lift up our cry to God, that he would return and visit the churches, and pour out a new, fresh, reviving spirit upon them, that we fall not under the power of these decays till we come to formality, and God withdraws himself from us, and leaves us; which he seems to be at the very point of doing.

Then, brethren, let us remember our own church; that God would in an especial manner revive the spirit of life, power, and holiness among us; that he would be pleased to help the officers of the church to discharge their duty, and not suffer them to fall under any decay of grace or gifts, unfitting of them to the discharge of their office to the edification of the church; that he would give them also to beware and take heed of formality as to the exercise of gifts in their administration; and that he would take care of us, since we are apt to fall under these things. Let us pray that we may be acted by the Spirit of God, and enlivened by the grace of God, in all things we do.

Have any of us any particular occasions in reference to temptations, trials, and troubles? — we may bear it upon our hearts to the Lord this day. This is much better than by multiplying a company of formal bills. The Lord help us to know the plague of our own hearts, and to be enabled to plead with the Lord, upon this opportunity, for grace and mercy to help us in every time of need!

IV. Recovery from Spiritual Decay[4]

QUESTION. *How may we recover from a decay of the principle of grace?*

ANSWER. We have been speaking concerning the decay of the principle of grace; and I will now offer you some few thoughts that may be applied unto our recovery from the decay of this principle. In doing which, I shall tell you no more than I think I have found myself.

If we would recover spiritual life, we must come as near as we can unto, and abide as much as we are able at, the well-head of life. Christ is the spring of our spiritual life; he is every way our life. It is in a derivation of life from Christ, and in conformity to him, that we must look for our spiritual life.

Before I mention how we should approach unto and lie at this well-head of life, let me observe to you this one thing, — that when there is a general contagious disease (the plague, or the like), every man will look to his health and safety with reference to other occasions, but will be most careful in regard to the general contagion. Now, if forsaking this spring of life be the plague of the age,

---

4 Delivered March 24, 1675-6.

and the plague of the place where we live, and the plague of Christians, we ought to be very careful lest this general contagion should reach us, more or less, one way or other. It is evident to me, — who have some advantage to consider things, as much as ordinary men, — that the apostasy, the cursed apostasy, that spreads itself over this nation, and whose fruits are in all ungodliness and uncleanness, consists in an apostasy from and forsaking the person of Christ. Some write of how little use the person of Christ is in religion; — none, but to declare the doctrine of the gospel to us. Consider the preaching and talk of men. You have much preaching and discourse about virtue and vice; so it was among the philosophers of old: but Jesus Christ is laid aside, quite as a thing forgotten; as if he was of no use, no consideration, in religion; as if men knew not at all how to make any use of him, as to living to God.

This being the general plague, as is evident, of the apostasy of the day wherein we live, if we are wise, we shall consider very carefully whether we ourselves are not influenced more or less with it; as where there is a general temptation, it doth more or less try all men, the best of believers, and prevail more or less upon their spirits. I am afraid we have not, some of us, that love for Christ, that delight in him, nor do make that constant abode with him, as we have done. We have very much lost out of our faith and our affections him who is the life and centre, the glory and the power, of all spiritual life, and of all we have to do with God, — Jesus Christ himself. I brought it in only to let us know, that if we would revive our spiritual life (and, believe it, if any of us are not concerned in our spiritual decays, these are sapless things, and will be heard with as much weariness as spoken), we are to abide more at the well-head of life. It is the direction of our Lord Jesus Christ, "Abide in me: unless ye abide in me, ye can bring forth no fruit. And every such branch shall be so and so purged."

But you will say, "How shall we do so? how shall we abide, more than we have done, at this well-head of life?"

1. We are to abide at the well-head of life by a frequency of the acts of faith upon the person of Christ. Faith is that grace, not only whereby we are implanted into Christ, but whereby we also abide in him. If so, methinks the frequent actings of faith upon the person of Christ are a drawing near to the well-head of life. And though we are to put forth the vigour, the earnestness, the watchfulness of our hearts unto obedience; yet a ceasing to continue in the acting of faith upon the person of Christ, even under the vigour of our own endeavours by those general, outward desires of walking with God and living to him, will weaken us, and we shall find ourselves losers by it. Do you all understand me? I am not teaching the wise and more knowing of the flock; I would speak unto the meanest. I say, suppose we should resolve with great earnestness, diligence, watchfulness, to abide in duties, in inward duties, to watch over our hearts, which is required of us; yet, if in our so doing we are taken off thereby from frequent actings of faith upon Christ, as the spring of our life, we shall decay under all our endeavours, watch-

fulness, and multiplication of duties. Wherefore, my brethren, let me give you this advice, — that you would night and day, upon your beds, in your ways, upon all occasions, have the exercise of faith upon the person of Christ; faith working by a view of him as represented in the gospel, by trust in him, and by invocation of him, — that he may be continually nigh unto you. And you cannot have him nigh unto you, unless you make yourselves, by these actings of faith, through his grace, continually nigh unto him: so you will abide at the well-head.

I could show you those excellent advantages that we should have by continually being near to Christ, who is the overflowing spring of grace, and from whence it will issue out to us, if we abide with him, be nigh to him, and keep up to this well-head.

2. Abide with him in love. Oh, the warm affections for Christ which some of you can witness concerning yourselves, — that your hearts have been filled withal towards Christ, when you have been under his call to believe on him! And it is a marvellous way of abiding with Christ, to abide with him by love; which is called "cleaving to God and Christ:" it is the affection of adhesion, and gives a sense of union.

"How, then, shall we get our hearts to abide with Christ by love?"

This is a subject that if I were to preach upon, how many things would presently offer themselves to us, from the excellency of his person, from the excellency of his love, from our necessity of him, the advantages and benefits we have by him, and his kindness towards us! All these things, and many more, would quickly present themselves unto us.

But I will name but one thing, and I name it the rather, because I heard it mentioned in prayer since I came in: Labour to have your hearts filled with a love to Jesus Christ, as there is in him made a representation of all divine excellencies. This was God's glorious design. It is not to be separated from his design of glorifying himself in the work of redemption; for a great part of God's glorious design in the incarnation of Christ, was in him to represent himself unto us, "who is the image of the invisible God, the express image of his person." Now, if you do but consider Christ as God is gloriously represented unto you in him, you will find him the most proper object for divine love, — for that love which is wrought in your hearts by the Holy Ghost, for that love that hath sweetness, complacency, satisfaction in it. Then, let us remember that we exercise our minds to consider Christ, as all the lovely properties of the divine nature and counsels of his will, as to love and grace, are manifested by Christ.

If we would abide at the well-head of life, we must abide in these things; and let love be excited to Christ under this especial consideration, — as he who represents the supreme object of your love, God himself, in all the glorious properties of his nature.

3. Add meditation hereunto; study Christ more, and all the things of Christ; delight more in the hearing and preaching of Christ. He is our best friend; let not the difficulties of the mystery of his person and grace deter you. There are wonderful

things of the counsels of heaven, and of the glory of the holy God, in the person of Christ as the head of the church; if you would be found inquiring into them, an unsearchable treasure of divine wisdom, grace, and love is laid up in Christ: therefore meditate upon them more. Let me assure you this will prove the best expedient for the recovery of our spiritual life. And I will abide by this doctrine to eternity, that without it we shall never recover spiritual life to the glory of God in Christ.

4. And then, brethren, seeing we have, in the next place, felt decays in the midst of the performance of multiplied duties, labour to bring spirituality into your duties.

"What is that," you will say, "and wherein doth it consist?"

It is the due exercise of every grace that is required to the discharge of that duty. Let every such grace be in its due exercise, and that is to be spiritual in duty. As, for instance, would a man be spiritual in all his prayers? — let him, then, consider what grace and what exercise of grace is required to this duty. A due fear and reverence of the name of God; faith, love, and delight in him; an humble sense of his own wants, earnest desires of supply, dependence upon God for guidance, and the like; — we all know that these are the graces required to the discharge of this duty of praying by the Holy Ghost. And let these graces be in a due exercise, and then you are spiritual in this duty. Is the duty charity, — giving a supply to the poor? There is to be a ready mind, a compassionateness of heart, and obedience unto the command of Christ in that particular. These are the graces required to the discharge of that duty, and to watch against the contrary vices. So that if we would bring spirituality into duty, it is to exercise the graces that are required by the rule to the performance of that duty.

I shall only farther give you this one caution, — have a care that your head in notion and your tongue in talk do not too fast empty your hearts of truth. We are apt to lay it up in our heads by notions, and bring it forth in talk, and not let it be in our hearts; and this weakens spiritual life greatly. Ye hear the word preached; and it is of great concernment what account we shall give of the word that hath been preached unto you: for we that preach must give an account of our preaching, and so must you of what you hear; and many a good word is spoken, truly, and yet we see but little fruit of it. And the reason of this is, that some, when they hear it, take no farther regard of it, but "let it slip," as the apostle speaks, Heb. ii. 1. And if we complain of the treacherousness of our memories, — it is the most harmless way of the slipping out of the word. It is not the treachery of our memories, but of our hearts and affections, that makes the heart like a broken vessel, — that makes all the rents in it where the water runs out, as the comparison is. The word slips out by putting your affections into carnal exercise; and it quickly finds its way to depart from the heart that gives it no better entertainment. We talk away a sermon and the sense of it; which robs us both of the sermon and the fruit of it. A man hears a good word of truth, and, instead of taking the power of it into his heart, he takes the notion of it into his mind, and is satisfied therewith. But this is not the way to thrive. God grant that we may never preach to you any thing but what we may labour to have an experience of the power of it in our own hearts, and to profit ourselves by the word wherewith we design to profit others! And I pray God grant that you also may have some profit by the word dispensed to you, — that it slip not out through carnal affections, and be not drawn out through notions and talk, with a regardlessness to treasure it up in your hearts!

These things we are diligently to attend unto, if we would recover our spiritual losses that we are complaining of, and that not without just cause.

V. THE GROUND OF AN APPLICATION TO CHRIST[5]

QUESTION. *It was queried by some, how we may make our application unto Christ; not in general, but under what notion and apprehension of the person of Christ?*

ANSWER. Because some seem to apprehend there might be danger in terminating our worship upon the nature of Christ as a creature, I shall give you my thoughts and directions in it. And, —

First. You must observe we are to have no conceptions, in our acting of any duty, towards Christ or about him, but with respect unto his person as he is God and man in one person. It is not lawful for us to have any apprehensions of Christ, to make any application to him, as man only; nor is it lawful for us to have any apprehensions of him as God only: but all our apprehensions of Christ, and all our addresses unto him, must be as God and man in one person. So he is, and so he will be to all eternity. The union is inseparable and indissoluble; and for any man to make his application unto Christ either as God or as man, is to set up a false Christ. Christ is God and man in one person, and no other. So, in all our actings of faith upon him, and applications unto him, we ought to

---

5 Delivered April 7, 1676.

consider him as he was "the seed of David," and as "God over all, blessed for ever," in one person. This makes the great idolatry among the Papists; — in the image of Christ they represent the human nature of Christ separated from his Deity; for they can make no representation of one that is God and man in one person: hereby they become guilty of double idolatry, referring the mind unto one that is a man, and no more, — and doing it by means of an image.

Secondly. The person of Christ is the immediate and proper object of all divine worship. The worship of Christ is commanded in the first commandment. By worship, I intend faith, love, trust, subjection of soul, invocation on the name of Christ, — every act of the soul and mind whereby we ascribe infinite divine excellencies unto God; which is the worship of the mind. See John v. 23. It is the will of God "that all men should honour the Son, even as they honour the Father." How do we honour the Father? By divine faith, trust, love, and worship; making him our end and our reward. So the Son is to be honoured. And as to the divine person of the Son of God, being of the same nature, essence, and substance with the Father, there is no dispute of that among them by whom his Deity is acknowledged.

Thirdly. The divine person of the Son of God lost nothing of his glory and honour that was due unto him by the assumption of our human nature. Though thereby he became the Son of man as well as the Son of God, — a Lamb for sacrifice; yet he is still, in his whole and entire person, the object of all that worship I spake of before; — and the whole church of God agree together in giving that worship unto him, Rev. v. 8, 9, 11–13, "And when he had taken the book, the four beasts and four and twenty elders fell down before the Lamb, having every one of them harps, and golden vials full of odours, which are the prayers of saints. And they sung a new song, saying, Thou art worthy to take the book, and to open the seals thereof: for thou wast slain, and hast redeemed us to God by thy blood out of every kindred, and tongue, and people, and nation. And I beheld, and I heard the voice of many angels round about the throne and the beasts and the elders: and the number of them was ten thousand times ten thousand, and thousands of thousands; saying with a loud voice, Worthy is the Lamb that was slain to receive power, and riches, and wisdom, and strength, and honour, and glory, and blessing. And every creature which is in heaven, and on the earth, and under the earth, and such as are in the sea, and all that are in them, heard I saying, Blessing, and honour, and glory, and power, be unto him that sitteth upon the throne, and unto the Lamb for ever and ever." Jesus Christ is here distinguished from the Father. There is, "He that sitteth upon the throne," and "The Lamb;" and he is considered as incarnate, — as a Lamb slain: and yet there is all the glory, honour, praise, and worship, that is given to him that sitteth upon the throne, the Father, given to Jesus Christ, God and man, the Lamb slain, who hath redeemed us with his blood.

Fourthly. This person of Christ, God-man, must not be so much as severed by any conception of the mind. For distinction, as God and man, he may be considered two ways; either absolutely in himself, or in the discharge of his mediatory office. And this double consideration produceth a double kind of worship to the person of Christ.

1. Consider Christ absolutely in his own person, as the Son of God incarnate; and so he is the immediate and ultimate object of our faith, prayer, and invocation. So that a man may lawfully, under the guidance and conduct of the Spirit of God, direct his prayer immediately to the person of Christ. You have the example of Stephen in his last prayer. "Lord Jesus," saith he, "receive my spirit." These were the words of our Lord Jesus Christ when he died, "Father, into thy hands I commend my spirit." And Stephen, when he died, committed his spirit into the hands of Jesus Christ: "Lord Jesus," (for that is the name of the Son of God incarnate, "He shall be called Jesus, for he shall save his people from their sins,") "receive my spirit." So that a person may make an immediate address in his prayers and supplications unto the person of Christ, as God and man. I look upon it as the highest act of faith that a believer is called unto in this world, — to resign a departing soul into his hands, letting go all present things and future hopes; to resign, I say, a departing soul quietly and peaceably into the hands of Christ. Now, this Stephen did with respect unto Jesus: "Lord Jesus, receive my spirit." There he left himself by faith. So we may apply ourselves unto him upon any other account, in the acting of faith, upon any other occasion.

2. Consider Christ in the discharge of his mediatory office. And under that formal consideration,

as discharging his mediatory office, he is not the ultimate object of our faith and invocation; but we call upon God, even the Father, in the name of Jesus Christ. "We through Christ have believed in God," saith Peter in one of his epistles. And it implies a contradiction to have it otherwise: for the calling him Mediator, showeth he is a means between God and us; and so it is contradictory to say our faith is terminated on his mediatory office. This he calls asking the Father in his name: "You shall ask the Father in my name;" that is, expressly plead the intervention of the mediation of Christ. And so the apostle tells us, in that grand rubric and directory of church worship, Eph. ii. 18, "By whom we have access by one Spirit unto the Father." The Father is proposed as the ultimate object of access in our worship; and the Spirit is the effecting cause, enabling us unto this worship; and the Son is the means whereby we approach unto God.

All that I shall add hereunto is this:— Seeing there is in Scripture a double worship of Christ that is immediate (for his person is considered absolutely, and as mediator between God and man), which of these ought we principally to apply ourselves unto?

I answer plainly, —

(1.) Our direction for solemn worship in the church generally respects Christ as mediator, in Scripture. The general worship that is to be performed unto God in the assemblies of the saints, doth look upon Christ as executing his mediatory office; and so our address is unto the throne of grace by him. By him we enter into the holy place,

— through him and by him unto God. "I bow my knees unto (God) the Father of our Lord Jesus Christ," Eph. iii. 14. God, considered as the Father of our Lord Jesus Christ, is the proper, ultimate object of the solemn worship of the church.

(2.) In treating and dealing about our own souls, under the conduct of the Spirit of God, it is lawful and expedient for us in our prayers and supplications to make addresses to the person of Christ; as Stephen did.

VI. How to Apply to Christ for Grace[6]

QUESTION. *How may we make our addresses to Christ for the exercise of grace; that is, that we may have grace strengthened, and be ready for all exercise? or, How may we make application to Christ, that we may receive grace from him to recover from decays?*

ANSWER. I think the direction given by our Saviour himself is so plain, and doth so fall in with our experience, that we need not look much farther. Saith he, "Unless ye abide in me, ye cannot bear fruit." The business we aim at is fruit-bearing; which consists as much in the internal, vigorous actings of grace, as in the performance of outward duties, — to be faithful in our minds and souls, as well as in our lives. "The way for that," saith our Saviour, "is, 'Abide in me.'" And unless we do so, he tells us plainly, do we whatever we will else, we "cannot bring forth fruit." So that the whole of our fruitfulness depends upon our abiding in Christ. There cannot, then, be much more said unto this business, but to inquire a little what it is to abide in Christ.

Certainly, it is not a mere not going off from Christ; as we say, a man abides when he doth not

---

6 Delivered April 19, 1676.

go away. For I hope that, under all the decays we have complained of, and want of fruitfulness, yet we have not left Christ, and gone away from him. We have so far abode in him as the branch abideth in the root, from whence it hath its communication and supplies. Therefore there is something in particular included in this abiding in Christ, dwelling in Christ, and Christ dwelling in us.

And there seems to be this in it, — that to abide in Christ, is to be always nigh unto Christ, in the spiritual company of Christ, and in communication with Christ. It doth not lie in a naked, essential act of believing, whereby we are implanted into Christ, and will not go from him; but there is something of an especial, spiritual activity of soul in this abiding in Christ: it is abiding with him, and in his presence.

And as this abiding with Christ must be by some acts of our souls, let us consider what acts those are; which may give a little farther light into this matter. And, First, It must be, certainly, by some act of our minds. Secondly, By some act of our wills. Thirdly, By some act of our affections. And thus we abide with Christ; which is the way certainly to bring forth fruit.

First. There is an abiding with Christ in our minds. Now this, to me, is in contemplation and thoughts of him night and day, — "I sought him on my bed, in the night," saith the spouse; — to consider very much the person of Christ, to contemplate upon him as vested with his glorious office, and as intrusted and designed by the Father to this work. "We all," saith the apostle, "with open face beholding the glory of the Lord as in a glass, are changed into the same image from glory to glory, by the Spirit of the Lord." My brethren, that which you and I are aiming at is, to be "changed into the same image;" that is, into the image and likeness of the glory of God in Christ. I dare boldly say, by those of us who have reason to have daily apprehensions of our going out of the world, and leaving this state of things, that we have no greater desire, nor is there any thing more frequent in our minds, than this, that we may be more and more changed into that image before we go out of this world; for we are looking after perfection in likeness to Christ. Therefore aged Christians especially will bear witness, that there is nothing now we long for more than to be more and more changed into the image and likeness of Christ. How shall we get to this? Why, saith he, "The way is, by looking steadily upon Christ, as a man looks with an optic glass to an object at a great distance. We behold him," saith he, "by looking steadily upon Christ himself, and the glory of God in him." Now there is a wonderful large object for us to behold; for when you look upon the glory of God in Christ, you have what you please of Christ for the object of your eye and view; the person of Christ, the office of Christ, the merit of Christ, the example of Christ, the death of Christ, and what you will, so you be much intent in your thoughts and minds, much in immediate contemplation about Christ. I do not know how you find it, brethren; but it is the advice I would give you who are aged Christians, and not likely to continue long in this world, to exercise yourselves in immediate contemplations upon Christ. All the teachings you have had from ministers, the principal end of them has been to enable you to this; and really, if I know any thing, we shall find them accompanied with a sweet transforming power, beyond what we have had experience of in other ways and duties. "We shall be changed into the same likeness."

Well, then, we abide with Christ in the acts of our mind, by immediate thoughtfulness and contemplation upon Christ in the night, and upon our beds, and in our walkings, and by the wayside, and in times we set apart for meditation. We are greatly to labour after an intuitive view of Christ; that is, a direct view in the contemplation of Christ.

Secondly. If you will abide with Christ, there must be an acting of your will in it also; and that is, in great diligence and carefulness about that obedience which Christ doth require, in all the instances of it. This is a great way of abiding with Christ, when we labour to have our wills in a readiness unto all the instances of obedience that Christ requireth at our hands. Let that be the question, whether it be the will of God that we should do thus, or not? And if it be so, pray let us be ready to show we do abide with Christ, by yielding cheerful and willing obedience to him in this instance and duty which he calleth us unto; and so in all other things. I would have every one of us think often of this matter, — what it is Christ requires of me personally, in a way of duty and obedience. And I would have us labour to have in great readiness all things which Christ requires of us. And especially, brethren, I would have this in a readiness, that Christ requires of me to walk very circumspectly and carefully, — to keep myself from spots and pollution, and defilements, by converse in the world. This Christ requires at all times, in all instances, and upon all occasions. What have we been preaching? what have former teachers been instructing us in? All that you are taught is, that you should come to the knowledge of all instances of duty, and the way of them, which Christ requires at your hands. And "if ye know these things, happy are ye if ye do them."

This is your fruit-bearing, — a direct contemplation upon Christ; wherein I would beg that both you and my own soul might be found more to abound, while we are in this world (and you will find Christ, in the discharge of this duty, will make very near approaches and frequent visits to your hearts, — more in the discharge of this duty than of any other); and to have our hearts in a readiness to comply with every instance of obedience Christ requires at our hands.

Thirdly. There is an abiding with Christ in point of affection. There may be love and delight in all these things; if there be not, very spiritual contemplations will be a bar. There is no duty that is required of any man in this world so spiritual, so heavenly, so evangelical, but, through want of love and delight, a man may be slothful in performing of it. I may tie myself to do so this hour or that hour, and have no benefit to my own soul, nor give any glory unto God, if there be not love and delight in it. They will sweeten the duty, and refresh the heart of God and man, Christ and us. So labour, brethren, and pray greatly for it, that you may abide with Christ with delight, that you may find a sweetness and refreshment in it, and that every season of retiring unto Christ may bring a kind of spiritual joy and gladness to your hearts. Now you have a great opportunity, having shaken off the occasions of life and other concernments, to dwell with Christ; — now it is a good time.

VII. ON FAITH AS TO THE ANSWER OF PRAYER[7]

QUESTION. *When our own faith is weakened as to the hearing of our prayers — when we ourselves are hindered within ourselves from believing the answer of our prayers, have no ground to expect we should be heard, or no ground to believe we are heard — what are those things that greatly weaken our faith as to the answer of our prayers; that though we continue to pray, yet our faith is weakened as to the hearing of our prayers? and what are the grounds that weaken men's faith in such a state?*

ANSWER. If our hearts are not duly prepared to the consideration of the great and glorious properties, presence, and holiness of God, and duly affected with them in our preparation for prayer, it is certain we can have no faith for the hearing of our prayers.

It is also of great importance that we consider aright in what state the things we seek for are promised; — whether temporal things, that are left to God; or spiritual, that lie under a promise, and so we may press God immediately about them.

There are two things that are certainly great weakeners of our faith as to God's hearing our

---

[7] Delivered March 22, 1676.

prayers:—

First. The one is, that intermixture of self which is apt to creep into our prayers, in public especially, in the congregation and assemblies. Self-reputation in the exercise of gifts, or whatever it be, weakens our faith as to the expectation of God's hearing our prayers.

Secondly. The other is, that we pray with earnestness and fervency, with noise and clamour of speech, but do not industriously pursue the things we pray for. Unless we watch and follow after these things, we shall not have ground of faith for the hearing of our prayers; — as, for instance, when the soul is burdened with a corruption, there is nothing we are more fervent in prayer unto God against; yet, when we have done this, we take no more care to get it mortified. Where is our faith that our prayers may be heard in this thing? We must pursue our prayers, or it will weaken our faith as to the hearing of them. We all pray; but do we believe that God will hear and answer our prayers?

I shall not speak unto the nature of that faith we exercise, or what assurance we may have of God's hearing our prayers; but I will tell you plainly what hinders in us the answer of our prayers:—

1. We are not clear that our persons are accepted. God had respect unto Abel and his offering, and not unto Cain and his offering. We can have no more faith that our prayers are heard than we have faith that our persons are accepted. How many of us are dubious, and know not whether we believe or no! or are the children of God or no! According as our faith is as to the acceptance

of our persons, so, ordinarily, our faith will be as to the hearing of our prayers. I do acknowledge that sometimes, under extraordinary darkness or temptation, whilst a person doth not at all know nor hath any assurance what is his own condition, — whether approved or rejected of God, — yet the Holy Spirit of God many times gives assurance of the hearing of that prayer which is poured out in the anguish of the soul. But let us bring things unto a good issue between God and our souls, and not complain that our prayers are not heard, when we are negligent to come unto the assurance of faith about the acceptance of our persons. We have had many days of prayer, and have not seen that return of our prayer that we designed. This evil lies at the bottom, — that we have been dubious as to our state of acceptance with God. Let us labour to amend it.

2. Another thing is this, — pray while you will, you will not believe your prayers are answered if you indulge any private lust, or do not vigorously endeavour the mortification of it, according to what the Scripture and duty require. If any lust ariseth in the soul, and we do not immediately engage to mortify it, as God requires, it will break out, and weaken our faith in all our prayers. Therefore, if you will be helped to believe the answer of your prayers, labour to search your hearts. Do not think that no corruption is indulged but such as break out into open sin. It may be you do not know the corruption you indulge; labour, therefore, to find it out, and you will find how your faith is weakened thereby.

3. Again; want of having treasured up former

experiences of the hearing of prayer. We have not provided as we ought in this matter. If we had laid up manifold experiences of God's having heard our prayers, it would strengthen our faith that God doth hear them. It may be some have prayed all their days; God hath kept their souls alive, that they have not wickedly departed from God, and they have obtained particular mercies; — why, such ought to keep a constant record of God's hearing their prayers. Every discovery made of Christ that draws our souls more to love him, and engageth us to cleave unto him, is our experience of God's hearing our prayers.

4. I might add, when we ourselves are not sensible that we arise unto that fervency of prayer that is required of them that believe. If we pray in the congregation, in our closets, or families, and when we have done, are not sensible that we have risen up unto that fervency that is required, we cannot believe our prayers are answered.

It is the duty of all men to pray unto the Lord; but it is incumbent on none more than those who have really and sincerely given up themselves unto God, and yet in truth have no comfortable persuasion concerning their condition. That is a state wherein I am so far from discouraging prayer, that it is your season for prayer in the whole course of your lives. When Paul was first called, before such time as he had evidence of the pardon of his sins, it is said, "Behold, he prays." If they truly attend unto their state and condition, they may be sure to be the persons of whom also it will be said, "Behold, they pray." And even in these prayers they may exercise faith, when they have not faith to believe that their prayers are heard. But while in this condition, it will be hard to believe that their prayers are heard, when they cannot believe that their persons are accepted.

VIII. When is Sin Habitually Prevalent?

QUESTION. *When may any one sin, lust, or corruption, be esteemed habitually prevalent?*

ANSWER. I shall premise some few things before I come to answer the question:—

First. All lusts and corruptions whatsoever have their root and residence in our nature, — the worst of them. For, saith the apostle James, chap. i. 14, "Every man is tempted of his own lust." Every man hath his own lust, and every man hath all lust in him; for this lust, or corruption, is the depravation of our nature, and it is in all men. And in the root and principle of it, it is in all men even after their conversion. So saith the apostle concerning believers, Gal. v. 17, "The flesh lusteth against the Spirit; so that ye" (believers) "cannot do the things that ye would." What doth the flesh lust unto? Why, it lusts unto the works of it. What are they? "Adultery, fornication, uncleanness, lasciviousness, idolatry, witchcraft, hatred, variance, emulations, wrath, strife, seditions, heresies, envyings, murders, drunkenness, revellings, and such like." The flesh lusteth unto all these things in believers, — the worst things that can be mentioned; whence is that [saying] of our Saviour, which yields to me a doctrine which is a sad truth, but so plain that nothing can be more. He foretells marvellous troubles, great desolations and destructions, that shall come upon the world, and befall all sorts of men, and says, "It is a day that 'as a snare shall come on all them that dwell on the face of the whole earth.'" Nothing makes me more believe that day, that terrible day of the Lord, is coming upon the face of the whole earth, than this, that it comes "as a snare." "Men do not take notice of it; do you, therefore, take heed to yourselves, you that are my disciples: believers, 'take heed to yourselves, lest at any time your hearts be overcharged with surfeiting, and drunkenness, and the cares of this life, and so that day come upon you at unawares.'" The doctrine I observe from thence is this, — that the best of men have need to be warned to take care of the worst of sins in the approach of the worst of times. Who would think, when such troubles, distresses, desolations, were coming upon a nation, in that place the disciples of Christ should be in danger of being overtaken with surfeiting, and drunkenness, and the cares of this life? Yet he who is the wisdom of God, knew how it would be with us. Nay, what if a man should say, from observation, that professors are never more in danger of sensual, provoking sins, than when destruction is lying nearest at the door? "In that day," saith he, "take care."

Secondly. Another thing I would premise is this, — that this root of sin abiding in us, as I have showed, will, upon its advantage, work unto all sorts of evils; — which should give us a godly jealousy over our souls, and over one another. Saith the apostle, Rom. vii. 8, "Sin wrought in me all manner of concupiscence."

Thirdly. If it be so, that sin doth thus always abide in us, and will upon occasions work to all its fruit, to all manner of concupiscence, then the mortification of sin is a continual duty, that we ought to be exercised in all our days. Col. iii. 3, "Ye are dead, and your life is hid with Christ in God." A blessed state and condition! I desire no better attainment in this world than this holds out. But what duty does the apostle infer from thence? "Therefore," saith he, "mortify your members which are upon the earth." What, I pray? "Fornication, uncleanness, inordinate affection, evil concupiscence, and covetousness, which is idolatry." The mortification of sin is a duty incumbent upon the best of saints.

Fourthly. The fourth thing I would premise is this, — that a particular sin doth not obtain a signal prevalency without it hath some signal advantage; for our corrupt nature is universally and equally corrupt; but a particular sin obtains prevalency by particular advantages.

It would be too long to speak of all those advantages. I shall name two, whereunto others may be reduced:—

1. The inclination of constitution gives particular advantages unto particular sins. Some may be very much inclined to envy; some to wrath and passion; and others to sensual sins, — gluttony, drunkenness, uncleanness, — to name the things which our Saviour names, and warns us of. It is with respect hereunto that David said he "would keep himself from his iniquity," as some think. I

have only this to say, — that it hath been much from the fallacy of the devil that men have been apt to plead constitution and the inclination of their constitution to the extenuation of their sin; when, indeed, it is an aggravation. "I am apt to be passionate in my nature," saith one; "I am sanguine," saith another, "and love company." They make their natural inclinations to be a cover and excuse for their sin. But this I must say, as my judgment, — that if grace does not cure constitution-sins, it hath cured none; and that we can have no trial of the efficacy of grace, if we have it not in curing constitution-sins. The great promise is, that it shall change the nature of the wolf and the lion, of the bear, the asp, the cockatrice, and that they shall become as lambs; which it can never do, if it doth not change it by an habitual counterworking of inclinations arising from constitution. If grace, being habitual, doth not change the very inclination of constitution, I know not what it doth. That is the first advantage whereby particular sins come to have signal advantage and prevalency.

2. Outward occasions; and I refer them unto two heads: —

(1.) To education. Particular sins get advantage by education. If we do even in education instruct our children to pride, by their fineries and deportment to themselves, — if we teach them to be proud, we heap dry fuel upon them, till such time as lust will flame. Let us take heed of this. It is an easy thing to bring forth a proud generation by such means.

(2.) Society in the world, according to occasion of life, is that which inflames particular corruptions. According as men delight in their converse, so corruption will be provoked and heightened by it.

I have spoke all these things previously, to show you where lies the nature and principle of the danger we are going to inquire into, and how it comes to that condition.

Now, I shall inquire a little into the question itself, — how we may know whether a particular corruption be habitually predominant or no?

Brethren, I take it for granted the vilest of those lusts which our Saviour and his apostles warn us against, to mortify and crucify, may be working in the hearts and minds of the best of us; and that a particular lust may be habitually prevalent, where, for particular reasons, it never brings forth outward effects: therefore, look to yourselves. I say, then, when the mind and soul is frequently and greatly, as there are occasions, urged upon and pressed with a particular lust and corruption, this doth not prove that particular lust and corruption to be habitually prevalent; for it may be a temptation. This may all proceed from the conjunction of temptation with indwelling sin; which will make it fight and war, and use force, and lead captive.

But suppose a person be in that condition, how shall he know whether it be a temptation in conjunction with indwelling sin in general, or whether it be an habitual prevalency of a particular corruption?

I answer, —

I. It is not from the prevalency of corruption these three ways:—

1. If the soul be more grieved with it than de-

filed by it, it is a temptation, and not a lust habitually prevalent. In this case, when a heart is so solicited with any sin, sin and grace are both at work, and have their contrary aims. The aim of grace is to humble the soul; and the aim of sin, to defile it. And the soul is so far defiled as, by the deceitfulness and solicitations of sin, consent is obtained. Defilement ariseth not from temptation as active upon the mind, but from temptation as admitted with consent: so far as it consents, whether by surprisal or long solicitations, so far it is defiled. It is otherwise if the soul be more grieved with it than defiled by it.

2. It is so, when the soul can truly, and doth, look upon that particular corruption as its greatest and most mortal enemy. "It is not soldiers who have ruined my estate, nor a disease that hath taken away my health, nor enemies who have ruined my name or opposed me; but this corruption, which is my great and mortal enemy." When the soul is truly under this apprehension, then it is to be hoped it is the power of temptation, and not the prevalency of lust or corruption.

3. It is so, also, when a man maintains his warfare and his conflict with it constantly, especially in those two great duties of private prayer and meditation; which if once the soul be beat off from, it is driven out of the field, and sin is conqueror. But so long as a man maintains the conflict in the exercise of grace in those duties, I look upon it as a temptation, and not an habitual, prevalent lust.

II. I shall now proceed to show when a corruption is habitually prevalent.

And here is a large field before me, but I shall

only speak some few things:—

1. When a man doth choose, or willingly embrace, known occasions of his sin, that sin is habitually prevalent. There is no man that hath the common understanding of a Christian, and hath any corruption or lust working in him, but he knows what are the occasions that provoke it. No man, unless he is profligately wicked, can choose sin for sin's sake; but he who knows what are the occasions that stir up, excite, and draw forth, any particular corruption, and doth choose them, or willingly embrace them, there is the habitual prevalency of sin to a high degree in the mind of that man, whosoever he be: for sin is to be rejected in the occasion of it, or it will never be refused in the power of it.

2. Let a man fear it is so, when he finds arguments against it to lose their force. No man is under the power of particular corruption, but will have arguments suggested to his mind from fear, danger, shame, ruin, against continuing under that corruption. When a man begins to find these arguments abate in their force, and have not that prevalency upon his mind they have had, let him fear there is an habitual, prevalency of his corruption.

3. When a man, upon conviction, is turned out of his course, but is not turned aside from his design, — when he traverseth his way like the wild ass, "In her occasion who shall turn her aside?" — if you meet her, or pursue her, you may turn her out of her way; but still she pursues her design. Men meet with strong convictions of sin, strong rebukes and reproofs; this a little puts them out of their way, but not from their design or inclination;

the bent of their spirit lies that way still; and the secret language of their heart is, "that it were free with me to be as in former days!" Certainly a corruption is habitually prevalent, if it seldom or never fails to act itself under opportunities and temptations. If a man who trades cheats every time he is able to do so, he hath covetousness in his heart; or if a man whenever opportunity and occasion meet together to drink, doth it to excess, — this is a sign of an habitual corruption, if he be not able to hold out scarce at any time against a concurrence of temptation and opportunity.

4. When the soul, if it will examine itself, will find it is gone from under the conduct of renewing grace, and is, at the best, but under the evidence [influence?] of restraining grace. Believers are under the conduct of renewing grace; and I grant that sometimes, when, under the power of corruption and temptation, even they have broken the rule of renewing grace, God will keep them in order by restraining grace, — by fear of danger, shame, and infamy, — by outward considerations set home upon the mind by the Spirit of God, which keeps them off from sin: but this is but sometimes. But, if a man finds his heart wholly got from under the rule of renewing grace, and that he hath no leading or conduct but restraining grace, his sin hath got the perfect victory over him; that is, he would sin on to the end of his life, were it not for fear of shame, danger, death, and hell; he is no longer acted by renewing grace, which is faith and love, — faith working by love. A man who hath a spiritual understanding may examine himself, and find under what conduct he is.

5. Lastly, when there is a predominant will in sinning, then lust is habitually prevalent. Sin may entangle the mind and disorder the affections, and yet not be prevalent; but when it hath laid hold upon the will, it hath the mastery.

IX. Is Habitual Sin Consistent with Grace?[8]

QUESTION. *Whether lust or corruption, habitually prevalent, be consistent with the truth of grace?*

ANSWER. This is a hard question; there are difficulties in it, and, it may be, it is not precisely to be determined. I am sure we should be wonderfully careful what we say upon such a question, which determines the present and eternal condition of the souls of men.

Supposing we retain something of what was spoken in stating a lust or corruption so habitually prevalent, because this is the foundation of our present inquiry, I shall bring what I have to say upon this question to a few heads, that they may be remembered.

I say, then, —

First. It is the duty of every believer to take care that this may never be his own case practically. We shall meet with straits enough, and fears enough, and doubts enough about our eternal condition, though we have no lust nor corruption habitually prevalent; therefore, I say, it is the duty of every believer to take care this may never be his case. David did so, Ps. xix. 12, 13, "Who can understand

[8] Delivered April 19, 1677.

his errors?" saith he, "Cleanse thou me from secret faults. Keep back thy servant also from presumptuous sins: then shall I be upright, and I shall be innocent from the great transgression." He acknowledges his errors and sins, and prays for cleansing, purifying, pardon; but for presumptuous sins, sins with a high hand, and every habitual corruption, which hath something of presumption, — "Lord, keep back thy servant from them," saith he. The apostle's caution is to the same purpose, Heb. xii. 15, "Looking diligently lest any man fail of the grace of God; lest any root of bitterness spring up." There is the root of bitterness in every one; which I look upon as a corruption in some measure habitual, if it springs up unto great defilement. And I beseech you, brethren, beg of God, for your own souls and mine, that we may be careful this be never our case.

Secondly. The second thing I would observe is this, — whatever may be said concerning its consistency with grace, it is certainly consistent with peace. I wish we could remember what description was given before of this prevalent corruption, that we might consider the things now applied unto it. Here (though I would be as tender as of the apple of mine eye in these things) I will not fear to say this, that the peace which any one hath concurring with a prevalent corruption, is security, not peace. I know men may be at great peace under prevalent corruptions, and live upon good hopes that they shall be accepted with God, — that it shall be well with them in the latter end; and that they shall have power one time or other against this corruption, and will leave it when it is seasonable, and strive against it more than they have done: but all such peace is but security. Under prevalent corruption there is a drawing back; for I would state the matter thus: — a person who is a professor, and hath kept up to duties and obedience till some lust hath gotten strength, by constitution, temptations, or occasions of life, and hath drawn him off from his former renovation in walking with God; there is then a drawing back. Now, saith the apostle, "If any man draw back, my soul shall have no pleasure in him," Heb. x. 38. And when God hath no pleasure according to the several degrees of backsliders (it may be that is meant of final apostasy), he doth not intimate any thing that is a ground of peace to that soul. So Isa. lvii. 17, "For the iniquity of his covetousness was I wroth, and hid myself from him." If there be an incurable iniquity of covetousness, or any other iniquity, whether manifest unto us or no, God is angry, and doth hide himself from us. I pray, brethren, let us examine our peace; and if we find we have a peace that can maintain its ground and station under prevalent corruption, trust no more to that peace, — it will not stand us in stead when it comes to a trial.

Thirdly. The third thing I would say is this, — that if a prevalent corruption be not inconsistent with the truth of grace, it is certainly inconsistent with the true exercise of grace. It is not, indeed, inconsistent with the performance of duties; but it is inconsistent with the true exercise of grace in the performance of duties. It is often seen and known, that persons under prevalent corruption will multiply duties, thereby to quiet conscience, and to compensate God for what they have done amiss.

Persons may multiply prayers, follow preaching, and attend to other duties, when they use all these things, through the deceitfulness of sin, but as a cloak unto some prevailing corruption; but in all those duties there is no true exercise of grace.

The true determination of this question depends upon a right exposition of 1 John ii. 15. If we could understand that verse, it determines this point, "Love not the world, neither the things that are in the world. If any man love the world, the love of the Father is not in him." There is the question, whether prevalent corruption be inconsistent with true grace? I know the words may have this construction, "If any man do make the world his chiefest good, if any man put the world in the place of God, then the love of the Father is not in him; he hath either received no love from God, or he hath no love to God as a Father in Christ." But indeed the apostle, speaking unto believers, I am apt to think speaks not of the whole kind, but degrees, — if there be a prevalency of love of the world, there is no prevalency of the actings of the love of the Father, — that they do not concern the habitual principles of the love of the world, and of the love of the Father, but the prevailing actings of the one and the other. And, accordingly, it may be said of all other graces whatsoever, that where there is a prevalency of the acting of sin, there is a suspension of the exercise of grace. Brethren, if any of us have been under the power of prevalent corruption (I will be still tender, and speak what ought to be received and believed, whether people do or not), it is much to be feared we have lost all our prayers and hearing, because we have not had a true exercise of grace in them. Some exercise there may be, but a due and true exercise of grace will be laid asleep by prevalent corruption. And therefore let us take heed of prevalent corruption, as we would take heed of losing all things that we have wrought, — our praying, hearing, suffering, charity, — for want of a due exercise of grace in them.

Fourthly. I shall grant this, that spiritual life may be in a swoon, when the spiritual man is not dead. There is a kind of *deliquium* of the spirits, called swooning away, that may befall believers, which suspends all acts of life, when yet the man is not dead. So I say, though I should see a man, through the prevalency of corruption, have all the evidences of a spiritual life cast into a swoon, yet I will not presently conclude the spiritual man is dead. Take the case of David, from the time of his great fall and transgression in the matter of Uriah until the coming of Nathan the prophet. Persons are generally inclined to believe that the spiritual life was in a swoon, when the spiritual man was not dead. His fall, as an honest man said, beat the breath out of his body, and he lay a long time like a man dead, by reason of that power, which one signal sin left in his soul. And take that as a great instance that one sin, not immediately taken off by great humiliation, leaves great and even habitual inclinations in the soul to the same sin. So that some ascribed it unto the corruption of our nature. For it is a great and difficult question in divinity, how one particular sin, as the sin of Adam was, should bring in habitual corruption to our nature. To which some answer thus: That any one single moral act, performed with a high hand, hath great obliquity in it, disposing our whole nature to corruption. David, by that single act of flagrant wickedness, did continue in it for so long a space of time, till Nathan came and administered some good spirits to him, that relieved him out of his swoon. Wherefore I say that I will not judge a person to be spiritually dead, whom I have judged formerly to have had spiritual life, though I see him at present in a swoon as to all evidences of the spiritual life. And the reason why I will not judge so is this, — because if you judge a person dead, you neglect him, you leave him; but if you judge him in a swoon, though never so dangerous, you use all means for the retrieving of his life. So ought we to do to one another and our own souls.

Fifthly. There is a prevalency of sin that is inconsistent with true grace, which may befall those who have been professors. So the apostle doth plainly declare, Rom. vi. 16, "Know ye not, that to whom ye yield yourselves servants to obey, his servants ye are to whom ye obey; whether of sin unto death, or of obedience unto righteousness?" There is such a serving of sin as puts a man into a contrary state.

Sixthly. I shall add but one thing more, and that is this, — there may be a corruption, sin, or lust, habitually prevalent, as to whatsoever evidences the person in whom it is or others can discern; and yet the root of the matter, the root of spiritual life, be notwithstanding in the person.

Suppose, then, there be such a prevalency, that the soul judges to be habitual, how shall we know whether the root of the matter be in such a person or no?

If the soul hath any thing left of spiritual life, there will be something of vital operations in that soul. Now, the vital operations that give evidence the soul is not absolutely slain by prevalent corruption, are opposition and humiliation. So long as the soul, though it be never so much captivated, is conscious to itself of a sincerity in the opposition it makes, there is an evidence of a vital operation; as likewise where it is constant in its humiliation on that account.

But if it be farther inquired, how it may be known that this humiliation is sincere?

I answer, It cannot be known from its vigour and efficacy; for that overthrows the question. For if the opposition was vigorous and effectual, it would break the power of lust and corruption, so that it would be no more prevalent. But two ways it may be known.

1. By its constancy. If the root of the matter be still in us, there will be a constant opposition to every act of any prevailing corruption whatsoever. I do not speak about violent temptations, but ordinary cases; in which I know not whence we should conclude the root of the matter is in that man who doth not make a sincere opposition to every instance of the acting of prevalent corruption. If a man can pass over one and another instance of prevalent corruption without any humiliation for it, the holy, sovereign God show him grace and mercy! but it is to me "the way of a serpent upon a stone," — I see it not, I know it not.

2. It is sincere, if it be from its proper spring; that is, if the opposition be not from conviction,

light, or conscience only, but from the will of the poor sinner. "I would do otherwise; I would have this sin destroyed, — I would have it rooted out, that it should be no more in me; my will lies against it, however it hath captivated my affections and disturbed my course."

This is all I dare say upon this question, — that there may be an habitual prevalency of corruption, which may seem so to them in whom it is, as also to those who converse with them, and yet the root of the matter be in them. We may know the root of the matter by the acting of spiritual life, — in opposition going before, and humiliation coming after. We may know the sincerity of these vital actings by their constancy, and by their spring, — if we are constant in them, and if they arise from our wills.

X. How to Deal with Prevailing Sin[9]

QUESTION. *What shall a person do who finds himself under the power of a prevailing corruption, sin, or temptation?*

ANSWER. I shall premise only this one thing, and then inquire whether it belongs to us or no:—

This prevalency hath many degrees. It may be a prevalency to outward scandal, or to the utter loss of inward peace, or to the disquieting and divesting of us of that tranquillity of mind usually which Christ calleth us unto. Now, pray consider that I speak to it equally and in every degree. And perhaps there may be none of us but, at one time or other, after inquiry, will have had experience in one degree or other, either to disquietment, loss of peace, or scandal.

What shall such a person then do, who finds it so with him?

I answer, —

First. He should labour to affect his mind with the danger of it. It is not conceivable how subtle sin is to shift off an apprehension of the danger of it. "Notwithstanding this," says the man, "yet I hope I am in a state of grace, and shall be saved,

---

[9] Delivered May 4, 1677.

and come to the issue of it at one time or other;" and so the mind keeps off a due sense of the danger of it. I beseech you, brethren and sisters, if this be your condition, labour to affect your minds that this state, as far as I know, will end in hell; and let not your minds be relieved from the apprehension that, upon due and good grounds of faith, these ways go down to the chambers of death. Do not please yourselves, imagining you are members of the church, and have good hopes of salvation by Jesus Christ; but consider whither this tends, and affect your minds with it.

Secondly. When the person is affected with the danger of it, the next thing to be done is, to burden his conscience with the guilt of it. For the truth is, as our minds are, upon many pretences, slow to apprehend the danger of sin; so our consciences are very unwilling to take the weight of the burden of it as to its guilt. I speak not of men of seared consciences, that, lay what weight you will upon them, will feel none; but even of the consciences of renewed men, unless they use all the ways and means whereby conscience may be burdened, — as by apprehensions of the holiness of God, of the law, of the love of Christ, and of all those things whereby conscience must be made to feel the weight of its guilt. No sooner doth it begin to be made a little sick with a sense of the guilt of sin, but it takes a cordial presently. "Here this sin hath taken place, it hath contracted this and that guilt; I have been thus long negligent in this or that duty; I have thus long engaged in this and that folly, and been so given up unto the world: I must take to Christ by faith, or I am undone." It is afraid of making its load. But let conscience bear the burden, and not easily shift it off, unless it can, by true faith, guided by the word, load it upon Christ; which is not a thing of course to be done.

Thirdly. "What shall we do in case we have this apprehension of its danger, and can be thus burdened with its guilt?" Pray for deliverance. "How?" you will say. There is in the Scriptures mention of "roaring," Ps. xxxii. 3, "The voice of my roaring;" and likewise of "shouting," Lam. iii. 8, "I shouted and cried." This is a time to pray that God would not hide his face from our roaring, nor shut out our prayers when we shout unto him; that is, to cry out with all the vigour of our souls. Christ is able "to succour" and help them that "make an outcry" to him. The word signifies so;[10] and our word "succour," signifies a running in to help a man who is ready to be destroyed. These may seem hard things to us, but it is a great thing to save our souls, and to deliver ourselves from the snares of Satan.

Fourthly. Treasure up every warning, and every word that you are convinced was pointed against your particular corruption. There is none of you who may have the power of particular corruptions, but God, at one time or other, in his providence or word, gives particular warning, that the soul may say, "This is for me, I must comply with it;" but "it is like a man that sees his face in a glass, and goes away, and immediately forgets what manner of man he was," — there is an end of it. But if God give you such warnings, set them

---

10 Βοηθέω, (Βοή, θέω), to run in answer to a cry for help, Heb. ii. 18. — Ed.

down, treasure them up, lose them not; they must be accounted for. "He that, being often reproved, hardens his neck, shall suddenly be destroyed, and that without remedy."

Fifthly. I shall mind you of two rules, and so have done:—

1. In your perplexities as to the power of sin, exercise faith, that, notwithstanding all you see and find that you are almost lost and gone, there is a power in God, through Christ, for the subduing and conquering of it.

2. It is in vain for any to think to mortify a prevailing sin, who doth not at the same time endeavour to mortify all sin, and to be found in every duty. Here is a person troubled and perplexed with a temptation or corruption; both are the same in this case: he cries, "O that I were delivered! I had rather have deliverance than life! I will do my endeavour to watch against it." But it may be this person will not come up to a constancy in secret prayer; — he will go up and down, and wish himself free, but will not be brought up to such duties [as] wherein those lusts must be mortified. Therefore, take this rule along with you, — never hope to mortify any corruption whereby your hearts are grieved, unless you labour to mortify every corruption by which the Spirit of God is grieved; and be found in every duty, especially those under which grace thrives and flourishes.

XI. Christian Duty in Dark Dispensations

QUESTION. *What is our duty with respect to dark and difficult dispensations of God's providence in the world?*

ANSWER. In answer unto this question, three things are to be considered:— First. What are, in a Scripture sense, those things that make a season of providence dark and difficult? Secondly. What are the open signs of the coming and passing of such a season over us? And, Thirdly. What are our special duties in reference to our entering into, and passing through, such a season?

First. What are those things that make a season of providence dark and difficult?

I find four things in Scripture that make a dark season of providence; and, if I mistake not, they are all upon us:—

1. The long-continued prosperity of wicked men. This you are sensible is the most known case of all the Old Testament, Ps. lxxiii.; Jer. xii. 1–3; Hab. i. 4, 13, and many other places. The holy men of old did confess themselves in great perplexity at the long-continued prosperity of wicked men, and their long-continued prosperity in ways of wickedness. Give but this one farther circumstance to it, — the long-continued prosperity of wicked men

in their wickedness, when the light shines round about them to convince them of that wickedness, and God speaks in and by the light of his word against them; that is a trial. When all things were wrapped up in darkness and idolatry, it is no wonder at the patience of God; but when things come in any place to that state that many continue prosperous in wickedness when the day is upon them that judges them, — it is a difficulty.

2. It is a difficult season of providence, when the church is continued under persecution and distress in a time of prayer, when they give themselves to prayer. The difficulty seems mentioned, Ps. lxxx. 4, "O LORD, how long wilt thou smoke against the prayer of thy people?" This made it hard, that God should afflict his church, and keep her under distresses, and suffer the furrows to be made long upon her back, and continue her under oppression from one season to another. There may be evident reason for that. But saith God, "Call upon me in the time of trouble, and I will hear." God hath promised to hear the church: Will not God avenge the elect, that call upon him day and night? He will do it speedily. Now, when God seems to be angry with the prayers of his people, that is a difficult season: when they cry and shout, and God shuts out their prayers, that makes a dark providence.

As the other difficulty is evidently upon us, so I hope we have this difficulty to conflict withal, that the anger of God continues to smoke against the prayers of his people, as having stirred up many a blessed cry to himself; for there is a time when he will hear and answer their prayers.

3. It is a dark and difficult dispensation of providence, when the world and nations of the world are filled with confusion and blood, and no just reason appearing why it should be so. When our Saviour foretells a difficult season, Matt. xxiv. and Luke xxi., he says, "There shall be terrible times, such as never were; nation shall rise against nation, and kingdom against kingdom; and there shall be wars, bloodshed, and earthquakes; and the very elect shall hardly escape." Therefore God calls such a time, "a day of darkness," yea, of "thick darkness," Joel ii. 2, a dark, gloomy day. There is nothing to be seen in all the confusions that are in the world at this day, but that the frogs or unclean spirits are gone forth to stir up the lusts of men to make havoc of one another.

4. It adds greatly to the difficulty of a season, when we have no prospect whither things are tending, and what will be their issue.

There are two ways whereby we may have a prospect of things that are in being: — by the eye of God's providence, when we perceive which way that looks; and by Scripture rule. The truth is, we are in a time wherein no man can discern a fixed eye of providence looking this way or that way. What will be the issue of these things; whether it will be the deliverance of the church, or the desolation of the nation and straitening of the church; whether God will bring good out of them in this generation, or any other time, none knows: this makes it difficult. Ps. lxxiv. 9, We see not our signs, — have no tokens what God intends to do; "neither is there among us any to tell us how long."

There is none of these things but make a season difficult, and providence dark; but when all of them concur together, they cannot but greatly heighten it: and I think they are all upon us.

Secondly. What are the open signs of the coming and passing of such a season over us?

There are three tokens or outward evidences of a difficult season. It is so, —

1. When God's patience is abused. You know that place, Eccles. viii. 11, "Because sentence against an evil work is not executed speedily, therefore the heart of the sons of men is fully set in them to do evil." Things pass thus:— men fall into wickedness, great wickedness; their consciences fly in their faces, and they are afraid; the power of their lusts carries them into the same wickedness again, and their consciences begin to grow a little colder than they were: no evil comes of it, and judgment is not speedily executed; and so their hearts at last come to be wholly set to do evil. Hence others that look on say, "Here are men given up to all wickedness; surely judgment will speedily come upon these men." Judgment doth not come, — God is patient; and so they themselves turn as wicked as the former. Abusing of God's patience is an evident sign of a dispensation of the displeasure of God in his providence: and if ever it was upon any, it is upon us; and men learn it more and more every day. Every one talks of other men's sins; and seeing no judgment falls upon them, they give up themselves to the same sins.

2. It is so when God's warnings are despised: "When thine hand is lifted up, they will not see." That is a difficult season; for, saith God, "The fire of thine adversaries shall consume thee." Nev-

er had people more warnings than we have had; — warning in heaven above, and warning on the earth beneath; warnings by lesser judgments, and warnings by greater; and warnings by the word. God's hand hath been lifted up; but who takes notice of it? Some despise it, and others talk of it as a tale to be told; and there is an end of it. Who sanctifies the name of God in all the warnings that are given us? "The LORD's voice crieth unto the city," Mic. vi. 9; but it is only "the man of wisdom," of substance, that seeth the name of God in these his cries unto the city by his warnings from heaven and earth, signs and tokens, and great intimations of his displeasure.

3. An inclination in all sorts of people to security, and to take no notice of these things. I have spoken unto this business of security formerly, and I pray God warn you and myself of it; for I believe none of us are such strangers to our hearts, but we can say, that under all these warnings there is an inclination to security: if God did not prevent it, we should fall fast asleep under all the judgments that are round about us.

Any of these things shows that we are under a difficult dispensation of providence; but where all concur, — God be merciful to such a people! — it is the opening of the door to let out judgments to the uttermost.

Now if this be such a season, as I do verily believe we are all sensible it is, then, —

Thirdly, What shall we do? what are our special duties in reference to our entering into, and passing through, such a season?

I might speak unto the peculiar exercise of

those graces which are required unto such a season; as faith, resignation to the will of God, readiness for his pleasure, waiting upon God, weanedness from the world, and the like; but I will only give you three or four duties, which are peculiarly hinted in such a season, and so have done:—

1. Our first duty is, that we should meet together, and confer about these things, Mal. iii. 16, 17. A good plan in difficult seasons, such as some of us have seen. The day of the Lord was coming that would burn as an oven: "Then they that feared the LORD spake often one to another: and the LORD hearkened, and heard it, and a book of remembrance was written before him for them that feared the LORD, and that thought upon his name. And they shall be mine, saith the LORD of hosts, in that day when I make up my jewels; and I will spare them, as a man spareth his own son that serveth him." When was this? In a time of great judgment, and great sin, — "when they called the proud happy, and they that wrought wickedness were set up, and they that tempted God were even delivered;" that is, "appeared to be delivered." It is the great duty of us all, as we have opportunity and occasion, to confer about these things; about the causes of them, — what ariseth from the profane, wicked world; what from a persecuting, idolatrous world; and (wherein we are more concerned) what from a professing generation; and see how we can sanctify the name of God in it. We might have as great advantages as any under the face of heaven for the discharge of this duty, if we did but make use of that "price" [Prov. xvii. 16] which God hath put into our hands; but if we

are "fools," and have no "heart" to improve it, the blame will be our own. You have opportunities for meeting and assembling: I fear there are cold affections in your private meetings; I wish there be not. It may be some thrive and grow; I hope so: and others are cold and backward; it is not a season for it. If God would help us to manage this church aright, and as we ought to do, there can be no greater advantage under such a season than we enjoy: but we want voluntary inspection; and the Lord lay it not to our charge we have deferred it so long. Much want of love might have been prevented, many duties furthered, and many evils removed, if we had come up to the light God hath given to us. But we are at a loss; and God knows we suffer under it, for want of discharging our duty.

That is the first thing, — to speak often one to another; — to sanctify the name of God by an humble, diligent inquiry into the causes of these dispensations, and preparation for these things.

2. The second duty in such a season is, for every one of us privately to inquire of Jesus Christ, in prayer and supplication, "What shall be the end of these things?" You have a great instance of it, Dan. viii. 13, 14, "Then I heard one saint speaking, and another saint said unto that certain saint which spake, How long shall be the vision concerning the daily sacrifice, and the transgression of desolation, to give both the sanctuary and the host to be trodden under foot? And he said unto me, Unto two thousand and three hundred days; then shall the sanctuary be cleansed." I suppose there is something of the ministry of angels in it; for this saint

inquires, but the answer is made to Daniel, "One saint said unto another saint;" — "and he said unto me." But the speaking saint was Jesus Christ. There was the Holy One that spake, which he calls פַּלְמוֹנִי, "a certain saint;" but the derivation of the word is, "One that revealeth secrets."[11] There was application made unto Jesus Christ, who is the revealer of secrets, to know how long. And you will find in the Scriptures, in difficult dispensations, that is very many times the request of the saints to God, "How long?" Dan. xii. 6, 8, "How long shall it be to the end of these wonders?" and, "O my Lord, what shall be the end of these things?" There is an humble application by faith and prayer unto Jesus Christ, to know the mind of God in these things, that will bring satisfaction in to our souls. Do not leave yourselves to wander in your own thoughts and imaginations. It is impossible but we shall be debating things, and giving a rational account of them; but all will not bring us satisfaction. But let us go to Jesus Christ, and say to him, "O Lord, how long?" And he will give in secret satisfaction to our souls.

This is the second thing, — frequently confer about these things; and press Jesus Christ to give your souls satisfaction as to these dispensations And then, —

3. Another peculiar duty required in such a season is, to mourn for the sins that are in the world. That is recommended to us, Ezek. ix. When

---

11 See this meaning supported in Willet on Daniel. The highest modern authorities consider the word as equivalent to two words combined, — viz., פְּלֹנִי — *an individual;* אַלְמֹנִי — *one who is nameless.* — ED.

God had given commission unto the sword to slay both old and young, he spared only them that mourned for the abominations that were done in the land. We come short in our duty in that matter, — in [not] being affected with the sins of the worst of men. God being dishonoured, the Spirit of God blasphemed, the name of God reproached in them, we ought to mourn for their abominations. We mourn for the sins among God's people; but we ought also to mourn for those abominations others are guilty of, — for their idolatries, murders, bloodshed, uncleanness, — for all the abominations that the lands about us, as well as our own, are filled with. It is our duty, in such a season, to mourn for them, or we do not sanctify the name of God, and shall not be found prepared for those difficult dispensations of God's providence which are coming upon us.

4. The fourth and last peculiar duty which I shall mention is, to hide ourselves. And how shall we do that? The storm is coming; get an ark, as Noah did when the flood was coming upon the world: which is stated for a precedent of all judgments in future times. There are two things required to provide an ark, — fear and faith: —

(1.) Fear: "By faith Noah, being moved with fear, prepared an ark." If he had not been moved with the fear of God's judgments, he would never have provided an ark. It is a real complaint; we are not moved enough with the fear of God's judgments. We talk of [as] dreadful things as can befall human nature, and expect them every day; but yet we are not moved with fear. "Yet were they not afraid," saith Jeremiah, "nor rent their garments." Nor do we do so. Habakkuk, upon the view of God's judgments, was in another frame, chap. iii. 16, "When I heard," saith he, "my belly trembled; my lips quivered at the voice: rottenness entered into my bones, and I trembled in myself, that I might rest in the day of trouble." This is the way to find rest in the day of God's judgments. We are afraid of being esteemed cowards for fearing God's judgments; and then, —

(2.) We cannot well provide an ark for ourselves, unless we be guided by faith, as well as moved by fear. "By faith, Noah prepared an ark." How many things there are to encourage faith, you have heard; — the name, the properties of God, and the accomplishment of the promise of God. By virtue of all those properties, encourage faith in providing an ark.

But you will say, "We are yet at a loss what this providing of an ark and hiding of ourselves is. 'A prudent man foresees the evil, and hides himself.' God calls us to enter into the chamber of providence, and hide ourselves till the indignation be overpast. If we knew what this was, we should apply ourselves unto it." I will tell you what I think in one instance:— give no quiet to your minds, until, by some renewed act of faith, you have a strong and clear impression of the promises of God upon your hearts, and of your interest in them. If it be but one promise, it will prove an ark. If, under all these seasons, moved with fear, acted by faith, we can but get a renewed sense and pledge of our interest in any one promise of God, we have an ark over us that will endure, whatever the storm be. Think of it, and if nothing else occur to you, apply your minds to it, that you may not wander up and down at uncertainties; but endeavour to have a renewed pledge of your interest in some special promise of God, that it belongs unto you, and it will be an ark in every time of trouble that shall befall you.

XII. Preparation for the Coming of Christ[12]

I DID at two meetings inquire among ourselves what was required in the time of approaching judgments and calamities, that the world hath been, and is like to be, filled withal? And God was pleased to guide us to the discovery of the necessary exercise of many graces, and the necessary attendance unto many duties, for that end and purpose. And we did design to spend our time this day to beg that God would give us those graces, and stir them up by his Spirit unto a due exercise; and that he would help us unto such a performance of those duties, that when the Lord Christ shall come, by any holy dispensation of his providence, we may be found of him in peace. That was the especial occasion of allotting the present time unto this duty; no ways excluding the reasons, occasions, and matter of prayer, which at other times we attend to for ourselves, the church, and the nation.

I would offer a few words that may stir us up unto this duty:—

The Scripture doth everywhere, upon all such occasions, call expressly unto us for a spe-

---

[12] Delivered March 14, 1678.

cial preparation, by the exercise of grace, in reformation and holiness: "Judgment must begin at the house of God;" and "what will be the end of them that obey not the gospel?" What, then, is our duty? Why, saith he, "Seeing that all these things shall be dissolved" (all this outward frame of things), "what manner of persons ought we to be in all holy conversation and godliness?" Brethren, we ought at all times to attend unto "all holy conversation and godliness;" but saith the apostle, "The approach of judgment is a peculiar motive thereunto; — 'seeing that all these things are to be dissolved.'" It is true, seeing Christ hath died for us, washed us in his blood, and given his Holy Spirit unto us, "What manner of persons ought we to be?" But the great motives are not exclusive of occasional exercises, but give an addition unto them. "Take heed that ye be not overtaken with surfeiting and drunkenness," — with any excess in the use of the creature. What if it be so? "Then that day will come upon you at unawares;" — the day when all shall be dissolved, — the day of judgment, — the day of approaching calamities. "You ought at all times to take care of these things; but if your minds are not influenced in the consideration of the approach of that day, 'you are not my disciples.'" I do not at all speak unto what preparations are required.

I could also reflect on those places where God expresseth his great displeasure against such who did not labour for a peculiar preparation upon approaching calamities. Isa. xxii. 12–14, "'I called for mourning, and fasting, and girding with sackcloth,' and you betook yourselves unto feasting on all occasions." "Surely, saith the Lord, this iniquity shall not be purged from you till ye die." And it is reckoned among the sins of the most profligate persons, that when God's hand is lifted up and ready to strike, they will not see, so as to learn righteousness, Isa. xxvi. 11.

Let us, therefore, beg for grace. Though God multiplieth warnings, makes appearances of mercy, and then writes death upon them, and entangles every thing in darkness, yet our work goes slowly on in preparation. Cry earnestly unto God for such supplies of his grace and Spirit that may effectually bring us unto him; that we may no longer abide in the frame wherein we are.

There are three things, and no more, that I know of (others may be named, but they may be reduced unto these three heads), that are required of us in reference unto approaching judgments; and there is not one of them through which we can pass, or which we can perform in a due manner, comfortably unto ourselves, and unto the glory of God, without we have some singular and eminent preparation for it. And they are these:— First. That we ourselves stand in the gap, to turn away the threatened judgments. Secondly. That we may be fit for deliverance, if it please the Lord graciously to give it unto us. Saith Christ, speaking of great calamities, "Lift up your heads; for your redemption draweth nigh." Thirdly. That we may cheerfully and comfortably go through the calamities, if they shall overtake us.

These three are comprehensive of all the threats of approaching judgments and darkness that encompass us at this day. Now, there is not one of them that we can be any way fit for, unless our hearts and lives are brought into an extraordinary preparation, according as God calls and requires. I do not know whether we believe these things or no, but they will be shortly found to be true.

First. Who dares among us to propose himself to stand in the gap, to divert judgments from the nation, otherwise than in a formal manner, who is not prepared by these things we have spoken of, and hath not some good and comfortable persuasion of his own personal interest in Christ, and hath not freed himself from those sins that have procured these judgments, and who lives not in a resignation of himself unto the will of God? who dares to do this? We shall provoke God, if we think to stand in the gap, and turn away judgments from the nation, when we see ourselves are concerned in procuring those judgments.

Secondly. We cannot be meet for deliverance, unless we are thus prepared. I have heard a notion preached and spoken upon other occasions, — which I confess I never liked, and the more I consider it, the more I dislike it; and that is, that God, in the deliverance of his people, works for his own name's sake, that he may have all the glory, — that it shall be seen merely to be of grace: and therefore he will oftentimes deliver his people, when they are in an unreformed and unreforming condition, that he may shame them and humble them by his mercy and grace afterward. I know no rule of Scripture upon which this notion may be grounded, nor one instance or example whereby it may be made out.

Here lies the truth of it, — when there are

two things concurring in the deliverance of the church, God will deliver them, notwithstanding all their sins and unworthiness, without any previous humiliation in themselves:— first, When God hath fixed and limited a certain season in his word and promise for their deliverance; and, secondly, When, antecedent unto their deliverance, they want means for humiliation. God delivered the children of Israel out of Egypt when they were in a very bad condition, — an ignorant, stubborn, faithless generation; but both these things were concurring:— God was engaged, in point of his promise, that, at the end of four hundred and thirty years, he would visit and deliver them; and they were deprived of all ordinances of worship in Egypt: not a sacrifice could they offer while they were there; not a Sabbath, I believe, though it is not expressed in Scripture, could they observe; — the way of worship and knowledge of God was taken from them. So, when God delivered the children of Israel out of Babylon, they were in no very good condition; but God was engaged in point of promise as to that time, that at the end of seventy years they should be delivered; and in Babylon they had no means for instruction or reformation, — no temple, no sacrifice; — these were denied. But whenever God doth afford unto persons all the means of grace for humiliation, reformation, and turning unto himself, — it may be as good as ever they shall in this world, — that God did ever deliver that people out of their distresses, when they refused to be reformed, humbled, or to turn unto him, neither instances of Scripture nor God's dealing with his church will make this good.

Therefore it is vain for us to expect any thing of this nature. If, indeed, for so many years we had been thrown into a wilderness condition, and had no preaching, no assemblies, no administration of ordinances, no warnings or charges from God, we might have expected the Lord would have given us deliverance; but to us, who have had all these things, and yet will not make use of what we have now at present, we have no ground to expect any such thing. Therefore I confess, neither by rule, instance, or example, do I expect deliverance, until God come in to work a thorough change and reformation in our hearts and lives; which makes it very necessary to be preparing to meet God in the way of his judgments.

Thirdly. The third thing that may lie before us is, how we may cheerfully go through the calamities which may overtake us. I will say no more unto that, because it is that which we did expressly insist upon in our former discourse. As to the best of us, who have been long in the ways of God, woeful will be our surprisal when the days of calamity come, if we have lived in negligence of complying with the calls and warnings of God that we have had, to bring ourselves unto a more even and better frame. We shall find our strength to fail us, and have our comforts to seek, and be left to inward darkness when outward darkness increaseth, and not know whither to cause our sorrows to go.

These things, brethren, I thought fit to mention unto you, that, if it be the will of God, they may be of use to take us off from those false hopes and false expectations which we are wonderfully ready to feed ourselves withal in such a day as this is wherein we live. It is high time for us to be calling upon God for this end.

XIII. THE CONTEST BETWEEN CHRIST AND ANTICHRIST

THE prophet Daniel tells us, when he understood by books — namely, the writings of the prophet Jeremiah — that the time wherein the great contest between Babylon and the church was to have its issue was come to a point, "Then," saith he, "I set my face to seek the LORD with prayer and supplications, and fasting." And if you will read his prayer, you will find nothing of confidence, nothing of self-ascription; but a deep acknowledgment of sin: "We, our kings, our princes, our fathers" (our church), "have all sinned;" so as that "to us belong shame and confusion of face." And never had such shame and confusion of face befallen the church as would have befallen them, if they had been disappointed in that trial. But he adds, "Unto thee belong mercies and forgivenesses." There he issues the whole business, upon "mercy and forgiveness," though he knew by books that the time was come.

Truly, brethren, we do not know by any Scripture revelation, as he did, that the time is come wherein the long contest and conflict between Babylon and the church will have its issue; but it looks like it in the book of providence, and so like it, that it is a plain duty we should give ourselves unto prayer and supplication, that it do not issue in shame and confusion of face; which belongeth unto us by reason of our sins. It is that contest which is now under consideration, and which seems to be coming to its issue, and all men are in expectation of it. It is the greatest, save one, that ever was; for the greatest contest that ever was in this world was between the person and the gospel of Christ on the one hand, and the devil and the pagan world on the other; and the next to that is the contest between Christ — in his offices and grace, in his gospel and worship — and Antichrist. And it is at this day upon its trial, in as signal an instance as ever it received. The question is, as to us and our posterity, Whether Christ or Antichrist? whether the worship of God or of idols? whether the effusion, and waiting for the effusion, of the Spirit of God in his worship, or all manner of superstitious impositions? This is the present contest; and, it may be, under heaven there never was a more signal instance of the issue of this contest than will be in these nations in these days; I do not say presently or speedily; but this, you all know, is our state.

I mention it only to let you know that there is more than an ordinary earnestness and fervency of spirit and wrestling with God required of us at this day for the cause of Zion, the interest of Christ, and defeating of his adversaries. What way God will work we know not. If he be at work, he hath said, that when a flood was cast out of the mouth of the dragon, to swallow up the woman everywhere (and we have had a flood cast out of the mouth of the dragon to swallow up the whole interest of Christ in this nation), the earth lifted up herself and helped the woman, and turned aside the flood. Good old Eli's heart trembled for the ark of God. The interest of God and the truths of Christ are yet among us, but hardly beset by the Philistines; and whether they may not take them I know not, — God only knows. But assuredly, brethren, our hearts ought now to tremble for the ark of God, that God would continue it among us, and not give his glory into the hands of the adversary.

I have mentioned these things only for this end, — that if God will, our hearts may be a little warmed, upon all occasions, in this great contest and conflict between Christ and Antichrist, to come in with our prayers to the help of the Lord, and of the ark of the Lord, — that we may see a blessed issue of this trial, and not be covered with that shame and confusion of face which belong unto us.

XIV. Christian Duty under Divine Warnings[13]

This meeting is for conference, and I would ask you a few questions:—

First. Whether do you think there are extraordinary calls and warnings of God towards this nation at this time?

Secondly. If there be, what is the voice of these calls?

Thirdly. Whether any sort of men, believers, or churches, are exempted from attending unto and complying with these calls of God? For there lies a reserve in our hearts. The nation is very wicked (I shall not repeat the sins of the nation), the warning is general to the nation, the body of the people, and God testifies his displeasure against them. Now, the inquiry is, Whether there be any rule that we, who profess ourselves believers, and a church, should count ourselves exempted from a particular compliance with these extraordinary calls of God, — that they are for others, and not for us? "If the scourge slay suddenly, he will laugh at the trial of the innocent," Job ix. 23. And the good figs went first into captivity.

Fourthly. What have we done hitherto in order

---

[13] Delivered February 15, 1680.

to it, that may evidence itself to be an answer to, a compliance with, these calls of God, which we have owned here before the Lord? We have been speaking of it, and it becomes me to judge that we have had good and sincere desires after it. And neither the church, nor any one in the church, shall have any reflections from me beyond evidence. It becomes me to judge that we have had in ourselves good intentions, and sincere endeavours after it, though they have been, it may be, no way suitable or proportionable to the present occasion; and therefore I must say, that, in an eminent and extraordinary manner, as yet we have done nothing. We have not consulted of it yet, what we should do, and "what it is" in particular "that the LORD our God requireth of us;" nor declared our designs and intentions for a universal compliance with these great calls of God for repentance and turning unto the Lord. I mourn over myself night and day; I mourn over you continually. I do not see that life and vigour in returning unto God, either in our persons or in our church relation, as I could desire. And give me leave to say, from an experience in my own heart, I am jealous over you. We may proceed to consider something of outward duties afterward; but as yet we are not at all come to it, but only to inquire into our hearts what we have done in compliance with these calls of God, in the reformation and change of our hearts, and vigour of spirit in walking with him. I speak it with all tenderness, that none might take offence; but I do acknowledge to you, that I have not myself attained, nor can I, though I am labouring to bring my heart to that frame which God requireth in us all at this time. I find many obstructions: if you have attained I shall rejoice in it with all my heart and soul; but if not, help them that are labouring after it. I intend no more at present but this, — to settle upon our souls a conviction that we have not as yet answered the calls of God in the heart: for if we have all apprehensions we have complied, the work is at an end.

I hope we may in due time go on to consider all the ways and instances whereby we may reform and return unto God; but in the meantime I offer this to you, — that unless the foundation of it be laid in a deep and broken sense of our past miscarriages and present frames, and I can see in the church some actings of a renewed spirit with vigour and earnestness to pursue our recovery and return to God, I shall much despond in this thing. But let us be persuaded that we are to lay this foundation (I desire we may agree upon this), that it is our duty to get a deep sense upon our hearts, as the first thing God aims at in his calls, of our past miscarriages, and of our present dead, wretched frame; in comparison of that vigour, liveliness, and activity of grace that ought to be found in us. Ought we not to lay the foundation here? If so, then we ought to apply ourselves unto it. It may be, though it be so with some, that they have such a lively, vigorous acting of faith in a deep and humble sense of their past miscarriages, yet it is not so with others; and we are looking for the edification of the whole. And therefore, brethren, do we judge it our present duty to labour to affect our hearts deeply with a sense of our present unanswerable frame unto the mind of God and

Christ, and of our past miscarriages.

If it be so, let us every day pray that God would keep this thing in the imagination of the thoughts of our hearts; not only of ourselves, but of one another. Observe the phrase of the Holy Ghost: when you come to "the thoughts of the heart," you think you can go no farther; but saith David, "I pray, O Lord, preserve this in the imagination of the thoughts of the heart of thy people;" that is, "in the first internal framing of our thoughts." There must be a frame acting and coining thoughts (if I may so say) continually in us to this propose. But I recommend this to you, — that if this be a truth, and we are convinced it is our duty to labour to affect our hearts with a sense of the unanswerableness of our souls, and the frame of our minds unto the will of God and the holiness of Christ, who is coming to visit his churches, — "What manner of persons ought we to be?" Not such as we have been. We should labour for a deep sense of this, and I hope it may not be unsuitable unto you; for if any of us have any corruption, temptation, or disorder in our spirits and ways to conflict withal, in vain, believe me, shall we contend against it, unless we lay this foundation.

I know one great means for the beginning and carrying on of this work, is by earnest crying unto God, — by prayers and supplications, and humiliations. I am loath to issue it there; I have seen so many days of humiliation without reformation, that I dare not issue it there: we shall make use of them as God shall help us. I desire the church would do so, if they find in themselves a sense of duty, and a heart crying to God in sincerity and truth. I have now been very long, though very unprofitable, in the ministration of the word; and I have observed the beginning of churches, and wish I do not see the end of them in this their confidence of mere profession, and the observation of these duties of humiliation. God knows, I have thought often of this thing; and I say I dare not issue it there. Let us have as many as we have hearts for, and no more; and as many as shall end with reformation, but no more. But let us all begin among ourselves; and who knows but that God may give wisdom to this church? I am ready to faint, and give over, and to beg of the church they would think of some other person to conduct them in my room, without these disadvantages. The last day will discover I have nothing but a heart to lead you in the ways of God, — to the enjoyment of God.

www.ingramcontent.com/pod-product-compliance
Lightning Source LLC
Chambersburg PA
CBHW011131070526
44583CB00023B/2990